Fact Finders®

PEOPLE YOU SHOULD KNOW

IRENA SENDLER

Get to Know the World War II Rescuer

by Judy Greenspan

Consultant: Mary Skinner, 2B Productions
Director and Producer of the PBS documentary
Irena Sendler: In the Name of Their Mothers

CAPSTONE PRESS
a capstone imprint

Fact Finders Books are published by Capstone Press
1710 Roe Crest Drive, North Mankato, Minnesota 56003
www.capstonepub.com

Library of Congress Cataloging-in-Publication Data
Names: Greenspan, Judy.
Title: Irena Sendler: Get to Know the World War II Rescuer / by Judy Greenspan.
Description: 1st Edition. | North Mankato, MN : Capstone Press, [2019] |
    Series: Fact finders. People you should know | Audience: Age: 8–9. |
    Audience: K to Grade 3.
Identifiers: LCCN 2019005993| ISBN 9781543571837 (hardcover) | ISBN
    9781543574654 (paperback) | ISBN 9781543571905 (ebook pdf)
Subjects: LCSH: Sendlerowa, Irena, 1910-2008—Juvenile literature. | World
    War, 1939–1945—Jews—Rescue—Poland--Warsaw—Juvenile literature. |
    Jewish children in the Holocaust—Poland—Warsaw—Juvenile literature. |
    World War, 1939–1945—Poland—Warsaw—Juvenile literature. | Warsaw
    (Poland)—History—Juvenile literature.
Classification: LCC D804.66.S38 G74 2019 | DDC 940.53/18092 [B]—dc23
LC record available at https://lccn.loc.gov/2019005993

Editorial Credits
Mari Bolte, editor; Kayla Rossow, designer; Tracy Cummins, media researcher;
Tori Abraham, production specialist

Photo Credits
Alamy: AF Fotografie, 24, Ceasar Cotting, 26, INTERFOTO, 5, Shawshots, 28; AP Photo: Alik Keplicz, 29; Getty Images: ullstein Bild, 9; Granger: 15, 17; Mary Evans Picture Library: Sueddeutsche Zeitung Photo, 21; Newscom: akg-images, 14, KATARINA STOLTZ/REUTERS, Cover, Underwood Archives/UIG, 12, World History Archive, 23; Shutterstock: Everett Historical, 19, piotrbb, 10, Roman Nerud, 7; Wikimedia: Image: Warsaw-Ghetto-Josef-Bloesche-HRedit.jpg, 18, Irena Sendler Gallery, 8

Source Notes
p. 9, line 10: Tilar J. Mazzeo. *Irena's Children: The Extraordinary Story of the Woman Who Saved 2,500 Children From the Warsaw Ghetto.* New York: Gallery Books, 2016, page 9.

p. 10, line 4: Ibid., page 10.

p. 17, line 4: *Irena Sendler: In the Name of Their Mothers.* 2010.

p. 18, line 2: Ibid.

p. 20, line 4: Dennis Hevesi. "Irena Sendler, Lifeline to Young Jews, Is Dead at 98." https://www.nytimes.com/2008/05/13/world/europe/13sendler.html. Viewed August 12, 2018.

p. 22, line 9: *In the Name of Their Mothers.*

p. 23, sidebar: Ibid.

p. 25, line 1: Ibid.

p. 29, line 6: Michael Fox. "Modesty is the M.O. For Polish Heroine Irena Sendler." https://www.jweekly.com/2011/04/22/modesty-is-the-m-o-for-polish-heroine-irena-sendler/. Viewed August 13, 2018.

All internet sites appearing in back matter were available and accurate when this book was sent to press.

Printed in the United States of America.
PA70

TABLE OF CONTENTS

1 EARLY MORNING ARREST

It was 3 a.m. on October 20, 1943, and Irena Sendler knew she was in trouble. She heard footsteps thundering up her stairs and fists pounding on her door. Irena lived in Warsaw, Poland, during World War II (1939–1945). Germany had conquered most of Europe. Now the dreaded **Gestapo** was about to break down Irena's door.

Less than five feet tall, Irena was a tiny woman with red cheeks and bright blue eyes. At 33 years old, she looked like a young mother. But Irena was a fierce fighter in the Polish **underground**, or the **Resistance**. When the Nazis took over Poland in September 1939, she joined other citizens who secretly fought back. For four years she outsmarted the Germans. But now the Gestapo had found her—and Irena had something to hide.

DID YOU KNOW?

The Resistance was made up of groups of people who secretly fought back against the Nazis. Their activities included spying, writing newspaper articles, fighting the Germans, and rescuing Jewish people.

By the end of 1939, there were about 140 secret resistance groups throughout Poland. Those who were caught could be questioned or tortured by the Gestapo.

Gestapo—the secret police of Nazi Germany

resistance—a secret group that fights against an enemy that has taken control of the area

underground—a group or movement organized secretly to work against an existing government

5

Irena ran to the kitchen. She grabbed a bundle of rolled tissue papers from her table. The papers were covered with the names of thousands of Jewish children Irena was hiding from the Nazis. If the Gestapo found the list, they would kill the children and everyone helping them. But where could she hide it?

The banging on her door was deafening. Desperate, Irena flung the roll of papers to Janina Grabowska, another Resistance fighter who was sleeping over that night. Janina swiftly tucked the list inside her shirt. The door crashed open and the Gestapo burst into the apartment.

DID YOU KNOW?

Anyone caught helping a Jewish person could be punished by death. Helping included hiding, feeding, or transporting them. Buying their valuables to give them money was also a crime.

The Nazis

Adolf Hitler was a German dictator and the leader of the Nazi Party. The Nazis believed their superior way of life was being threatened by non-**Aryans**, especially Jewish people. Hitler rose to power in 1933 by promising the German people a better future. He believed that Germany had suffered too much after World War I (1914–1918) and he blamed the Jewish people for all the country's problems. Hitler was an **anti-Semite**.

During World War II, the Nazis' "Final Solution" was to kill all the Jewish people in Europe. Hitler nearly succeeded. He was responsible for the deaths of 6 million Jewish people—including 3 million Polish Jews. This tragedy is known as the Holocaust.

anti-Semitism—prejudice or discrimination against Jewish people

Aryan—white northern European person considered by Nazis to be better than any other race

Irena Krzyzanowska was born in Warsaw, Poland, on February 15, 1910. When she was two years old, her parents, Stanislaw and Janina, moved away from the crowded city. The family settled in Otwock, a nearby village known for its tall pine trees and crystal clear air.

Janina and Stanislaw Krzyzanowska

DID YOU KNOW?

"I was taught since my earliest years that people are either good or bad. Their race, nationality, and religion do not matter—what matters is the person. This was one truth that was instilled in my young head."
　　　　　　—Irena Sendler

Stanislaw was a doctor. Many of his patients were Jewish and poor. At that time many Polish doctors would not treat Jewish patients. Considered outsiders and "different," Jews were often victims of **discrimination**, anti-Semitism, and violence. Irena's father wanted to help, not hurt. People were people, he believed. Everyone was equal. And he said so, even when many people around him disagreed.

"If someone is drowning, you have to give a hand," he taught his little girl. It was a powerful lesson Irena would never forget.

Otwock was founded in the late 1800s. Many Jewish families both settled in and visited the town.

discrimination—unfair treatment of a person or group, often because of race, religion, gender, sexual preference, or age

Irena, an only child, made many friends among her father's patients. They visited each other's homes and spoke Yiddish, a Jewish language, when they played. "I grew up with these people," Irena said. "Their culture and traditions were not foreign to me."

The family was happy in Otwock. But in 1916 **typhus** broke out in the village. Many of Stanislaw's patients got sick. While caring for them, he became sick as well. He died a few days before Irena's seventh birthday.

Otwock's mild climate attracted people interested in improving their health. Hospitals and sanatoriums were built to bring them to the town.

Irena and her mother moved back to the city. Irena made new friends, went to new schools, and studied to become a **social worker**. But she had learned her most important lesson in Otwock. Irena would never hesitate to help those who were drowning. And when Hitler invaded Poland, her helping hand would save thousands of Jewish lives.

DID YOU KNOW?

In 1931 Irena married her high school sweetheart, Mietek Sendler. Unfortunately it was not a happy marriage and they divorced after the war.

social worker—someone who provides financial or educational support to those who need it

typhus—an infectious disease characterized by a purple rash, headaches, and fever

WAR!

The Germans invaded Poland on September 1, 1939. Air-raid sirens wailed as terrified civilians ran for their lives. German warplanes bombed schools, apartment buildings, hospitals, and churches in Warsaw. Sometimes the pilots flew so low that Irena could see their faces. Tall buildings were turned into mountains of rubble. Bodies were piled in the streets. The city was without food, water, or electricity. Within weeks of the invasion, Poland surrendered.

Nearly 85 percent of Warsaw was destroyed by the end of the war.

Germany Invades

Two days after the invasion of Poland, France and Britain declared war on Germany. World War II began. The German and Polish armies fought viciously on the front lines. On September 17, the Soviet Union also invaded Poland. The country was outmatched. By the time Poland surrendered, 40,000 people were dead in Warsaw and another 70,000 on the battlefield.

The Nazis went on to invade Denmark, Norway, Belgium, the Netherlands, Luxembourg, France, Yugoslavia, and Greece. In every country, they rounded up Jewish people.

Everyone needed help. The new Nazi government allowed Irena and other social workers to help Polish people. But they did not allow them to help Polish Jews. So Irena did something simple—simple, but very dangerous. She made up Polish names for Jewish families.

When the Nazis checked her records, they saw nothing suspicious. But right under their noses, Irena and other social workers were bringing food, medicine, and clothing to thousands of Jews in Warsaw.

THE WARSAW GHETTO

Under Nazi rule Polish Jews soon lost their money and their jobs. They couldn't enter a park or sit on a public bench. They were kicked out of schools and beaten in the streets. They had to wear a blue and white armband with a six-pointed Star of David that identified them as Jewish. They were ordered to stay away from non-Jews. Anyone found with a Jew could be killed.

To visit her many Jewish friends in Warsaw, Irena took a risk and wore a Star of David to blend in.

In October 1940 the Nazis forced all Jewish families out of their homes. They were ordered to move to a tiny section of the city. This area became the Warsaw **ghetto**. A 10-foot- (3-meter-) high brick wall topped with barbed wire and broken glass surrounded the ghetto. Armed guards were on patrol. Anyone caught trying to escape the ghetto could be shot—even children.

Around one-third of Warsaw's population was Jewish. More than 400,000 people were forced into an area of less than 2 square miles (5 square kilomoters)—less than 2.5 percent of the city's area. As many as five families crowded into a single small apartment. Eight, nine, sometimes 10 people lived in one room. Disease spread rapidly. No one had enough to eat. Sick and starving, thousands would die each month.

Between 300 and 400 people died in the ghetto each day. Children could become orphans overnight.

The Ghettos

The Nazis first passed anti-Jewish laws in Germany. Then they passed them in every country they occupied. The laws were designed to separate, **segregate**, and isolate the Jewish population. The Nazis established hundreds of ghettos in Europe during the war. The Warsaw ghetto was the largest.

ghetto—area in a town or city where certain groups of people, such as Jewish people, were sent to live after being removed from their own homes

segregate—to keep people of different races apart in schools and other public places

15

To continue to help her Jewish friends, Irena needed to enter the ghetto. She knew the Germans allowed some health workers in. Someone in the underground got Irena special passes to distribute typhus **vaccines**. Irena and her friends went in and out several times a day. They usually dressed as poor, old women in heavy clothing. Nazi guards never suspected that they were smuggling meat, money, and medicine in their clothes. Sometimes Irena brought little dolls for the children. If she or her friends had been caught, they would have been arrested or killed.

DID YOU KNOW?

Terrified of becoming sick themselves, the Nazis allowed Polish doctors and nurses to go into the ghetto. Their job was not to save people from dying, but to prevent the spread of disease beyond the ghetto walls.

vaccine—a medicine that prevents a disease

The Nazis did not allow enough food to enter the ghetto. Many people starved. Between October 1940 and July 1942, 92,000 people died.

Inside the ghetto she saw Nazis kill and beat people for no reason. Bodies were hauled away in wagons. Barefoot children begged for a piece of bread. "I'd go out on my rounds in the morning and see a starving child . . . lying there," Irena said. "I'd come back a few hours later, and he would already be dead covered with a newspaper."

Soon Irena and her team saw that bringing in supplies was not enough. "Very quickly we realized that the only way to save the children was to get them out," she said later.

There was no time to lose. In the summer of 1942 the Nazis began emptying the ghetto. Every day they packed thousands of people onto cattle cars. Everyone—children, parents, grandparents—was **deported** to a death camp called Treblinka.

It took just two months to deport 300,000 people to Treblinka.

In August the order came to send orphaned children to the trains. It would take dozens of brave people on both sides of the wall to save their lives. But how could it be done? Irena Sendler would lead the way.

Death Camps

The Nazis built the first **concentration camp** in Germany in 1933. Thousands more were built during the war. In some death camps prisoners were forced to do slave labor until they died. In others they were sent to gas chambers. Deadly gas was pumped into sealed rooms, killing everyone inside.

Most prisoners in concentration camps were Jewish, but many were not. The Germans also rounded up political enemies and members of other groups they considered inferior. This included people with disabilities, Jehovah's Witnesses, German and Austrian Roma, and homosexuals.

concentration camp—a prison camp where thousands of inmates are held under harsh conditions

deport—to remove people from their homes and send to a concentration or death camp

5 > ESCAPING THE GHETTO

At first Irena's organization rescued mostly orphans. But when the deportations started, parents desperately handed over their children. "Those scenes over whether to give a child away were heart-rending," Irena later told a friend. "They ask if I can guarantee their safety. I have to answer no. Sometimes they would give me their child. Other times they would say come back. I would come back a few days later and the family had already been deported."

DID YOU KNOW?

Dr. Janusz Korczak was a well-known pediatrician and author of children's books. He also ran an orphanage for Jewish children. It was moved into the Warsaw ghetto in 1940. Despite offers to be taken to safety, he refused to leave his orphans. In August 1942 the 200 children in his care were deported. Korczak and his staff went with them. None of them survived the war.

Getting the children out of the ghetto was the next challenge. Climbing over the walls was impossible, but slipping under was one way to get free. Some children made a terrifying escape through the dark, filthy sewer tunnels. Others rode out in coffins headed to a cemetery. Some even went right past the armed guards. They were hidden in sacks, suitcases, ambulances, and coffins. They were buried under garbage or food. Children's mouths were often taped shut to keep them from crying. Babies were given drugs to keep them asleep.

Armed guards stood at the ghetto entrances. Anyone caught bringing things in and out of the ghetto without permission could be shot.

21

Once outside the walls, children needed safe places to hide. Catholic orphanages and convents helped. Other children were placed with foster families. Sometimes Irena and her friends took them in.

It was dangerous to hide Jewish children. They had to move often. If discovered, the Nazis would kill the children and their helpers. "Fear, and constant running away, and hiding became a way of life," one child remembered.

They had to hide their identities as well. Children were given new birth certificates and new Polish names. They learned Polish songs and memorized Catholic prayers. Remembering was a matter of life and death. Germans often stopped and ordered children to recite a prayer. It was a test the Nazis knew a Jewish child might fail.

DID YOU KNOW?

"I have to say that no work . . . was as dangerous as hiding a Jew. When you're hiding a human being . . . you have to realize you have a ticking time bomb in your home. If [the Nazis] find out they will kill you, your family, and the person you are hiding. How many people are prepared to take that risk all for a stranger?"
—Wladyslaw Bartoszewski, founding member of Zegota

Jewish children hidden at a Polish convent. One historian believes that as many as two-thirds of religious communities in Poland hid Jewish children and adults during the war.

Irena kept careful records of children's real Jewish names, their new Polish names, and where they were hidden. She and her friends continued to give money and aid to those hiding the children. She wanted to reunite families after the war too. The list was top secret. It protected the children's futures.

6

ARRESTED!

At the end of 1942, Irena joined a large underground network called Zegota. With its money and manpower she could save more children. But in October 1943 the Nazis arrested and tortured a Zegota fighter. The woman revealed Irena's name before she was killed. On October 20 the Gestapo broke down Irena's door.

Irena had a plan if she was cornered. She would toss her list of names out the window into her garden. Another Resistance member would find the papers later. Irena had practiced it many times. But it had a flaw.

Irena has been credited as being Zegota's main rescuer of children in the ghetto.

Irena remembered later, "I looked out the window. There were two Germans walking around. Nine were coming up the stairs. So my plan is out. Meanwhile they are breaking down the door and we are losing time. I had a split second to think and threw the list to Janina."

Janina hid the list under her shirt. The Nazis searched Irena's apartment for three hours. They tore apart the beds and slit open the pillows. They pulled up the floorboards and destroyed the cupboards. They found nothing but arrested Irena anyway.

DID YOU KNOW?

Irena never hid the list under the floorboards, or in the oven, or behind the wall. The Gestapo always searched these places. When she was arrested, she was hiding a large sum of Zegota's money. The Nazis never found it.

The German police used Pawiak prison in Warsaw during the war. In total, about 65,000 prisoners were brought there. Irena was locked up from October 1943 to February 1944.

For months the Gestapo tortured Irena and tried to make her talk. They broke her feet and her legs. Then they sentenced her to death. At the last moment, a Nazi guard let her go. Zegota had bribed him to free Irena. When the Gestapo found out she was still alive, Irena had to hide. But she continued saving Jewish children until the war was over.

Secret Identities

Keeping the names of Resistance fighters secret kept them safe. To protect the organization, members of Zegota pretended they were talking about a person named Konrad Zegota. The Gestapo was fooled and placed Konrad Zegota on their most-wanted list.

For safety Irena did not use her real name in the Resistance. Instead she was known by her code name, "Jolanta."

Janina took Irena's lists to another resistance group for safety. After Irena's escape the lists were buried in a friend's backyard. Unfortunately Warsaw was heavily bombed in 1944. Everything was destroyed.

When the war was over Irena and the friend reunited. They tried to re-create the names and locations of all the hidden children. They gave the names to the leader of a Jewish organization who was helping families find their children. Altogether Irena helped save 2,500 children.

7

WHEN SOMEONE IS DROWNING

After the war Irena was nearly forgotten. The new communist government in Poland buried her story for many years. But in 1965 Irena was honored by Yad Vashem, the World Holocaust Remembrance Center in Israel. She received a medal with the words, "Whoever saves a single life saves an entire universe."

As many as 1.5 million children were killed during the Holocaust. Of the 1 million Jewish children in Poland before the war, only about 5,000 survived.

Her Story Is Told

In the 1980s Irena visited Israel and met some of the children she had saved. In 2001 a group of Kansas high school students made Irena famous when they wrote a play about her life called *Life in a Jar*. It was performed all over the United States and in Poland.

Irena died on May 12, 2008. She was 98 years old. Today Irena's name goes hand in hand with courage and bravery. In Warsaw there are streets, parks, and even a type of tulip named after her. Her face is on coins, stamps, and city murals. But Irena never considered herself a hero. "I remember what my father had taught me," Irena said. "'When someone is drowning, give him your hand.' And I simply tried to extend my hand to the Jewish people."

GLOSSARY

anti-Semitism (an-ti SEM-i-ti-zem)—discrimination against Jews because of their cultural background, religion, or race

Aryan (AIR-ee-un)—white northern European person considered by Nazis to be better than any other race

concentration camp (kahn-suhn-TRAY-shuhn KAMP)—a prison camp where thousands of inmates are held under harsh conditions

deport (di-PORT)—to remove people from their homes and send to a concentration or death camp

discrimination (dis-kri-muh-NAY-shuhn)—unfair treatment of a person or group, often because of race, religion, gender, sexual preference, or age

Gestapo (guh-STAH-poh)—the secret police of Nazi Germany

ghetto (GET-oh)—area in a town or city where certain groups of people, such as Jewish people, were sent to live after being removed from their own homes

Resistance (ri-ZISS-tuhnss)—a secret group that fights against an enemy that has taken control of the area

sanatorium (san-uh-TOR-i-uhm)—an institution for rest and maintaining or improving health

segregate (SEG-ruh-gate)—to keep people of different races apart in schools and other public places

social worker (SOH-shuhl WUR-kur)—someone who cares for and is concerned with providing economic, educational, and other assistance to those who need it

typhus (TYE-fuss)—an infectious disease characterized by a purple rash, headaches, and fever; it is transmitted by lice, ticks, mites, and fleas

underground (UHN-dur-grownd)—a group or movement organized secretly to work against an existing government

vaccine (vak-SEEN)—a medicine that prevents a disease

READ MORE

Mazzeo, Tilar J. *Irena's Children: A True Story of Courage.* New York: Margaret K. McElderry Books, 2016.

Roy, Jennifer. *Jars of Hope: How One Woman Helped Save 2,500 Children During the Holocaust.* North Mankato, MN: Capstone Press, 2016.

Vaughan, Marcia. *The Story of World War II Hero Irena Sendler.* New York: Lee & Low Books Inc., 2018.

INTERNET SITES AND FILM

Life in a Jar: The Irena Sendler Project
https://irenasendler.org/

What Was the Holocaust?
https://www.theholocaustexplained.org/what-was-the-holocaust/

Yad Vashem: The World Holocaust Remembrance Center
https://www.yadvashem.org/

Irena Sendler: In the Name of Their Mothers. Dir. Mary Skinner. PBS. Accessed via Amazon.com.

CRITICAL THINKING QUESTIONS

1. Irena saved children at a great personal risk. Would you be willing to take the same risk? Why or why not?

2. After the war, Irena's work was forgotten. Only recently is her story being told. How else do you think people could learn about her work?

3. Do some research on how a democracy can be taken over by a powerful leader. Give some examples of modern-day nations in which something of this sort might be happening.

INDEX